PRACTICAL
JOKES

PRACTICAL
JOKES

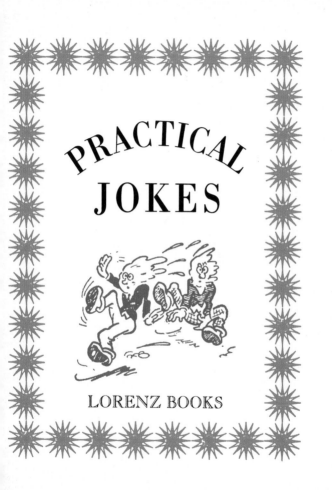

LORENZ BOOKS

This edition published in 1998 by Lorenz Books
an imprint of Anness Publishing Limited
Hermes House, 88-89 Blackfriars Road, London SE1 8HA

This edition published in the USA by Lorenz Books
Anness Publishing Inc., 27 West 20th Street, New York, NY 10011;
(800) 354-9657

This edition distributed in Canada by Raincoast Books
8680 Cambie Street, Vancouver, British Columbia V6P 6M9

ISBN 1-85967-769-X

A CIP catalogue record for this book is available from the British Library

Publisher: JOANNA LORENZ
Creative Director: PETER BRIDGEWATER
Text: PAUL BARNETT and RON TINER
Original Illustrations: IVAN HISSEY

Printed and bound in Singapore

1 3 5 7 9 10 8 6 4 2

The Publishers would like to thank all those who kindly
gave permission to reproduce visual material in this book;
every effort was made to identify copyright holders and
we apologise for any inadvertent omissions.

CONTENTS

NOTE
for the
CURRENT EDITION

*M*y great-uncle Freddie's small book Practical Joking for the "In", as by "Merry Freddie", was originally privately published in 1928, and distributed by him to friends and acquaintances. Within a year it was notorious among the smarter set. This had two consequences: his blackballing from several clubs, and the publication of a commercial edition, with considerable success, by Messrs Bartram Brothers & Co. The book went through eight editions in as

many months, and then – the shifts of fashion in those days being ruthlessly swift – was largely forgotten.

My great-uncle never married – perhaps unsurprisingly, given his fun-loving propensities. It was only in 1990, on the death of his rather grim niece Mildred, my late father's sister, that the rest of the family discovered in the attic of her Berkshire cottage, hidden away as if in shame, a box packed with unsold copies of each edition of Practical Joking for the "In". The book that you hold in your hands is a partial facsimile of the first (and fullest) edition.

The reason that the facsimile is only partial is simple: safety. Today, in a wiser age, publishers are more responsible than to promulgate the details of such devices as Molotov Porridge, Sulphuric Underpants, and Kippers that Glow in the Dark - the latter being safe in themselves, of course, unless eaten. The pranks contained in this version have been carefully selected for their relative safety. Nevertheless, it is as always true that fools can make danger out of even the most innocent of ingredients.

For my own part, I trust that no one will perform these tricks at all. Indeed, I rue the fact that this facsimile edition must be published, but the wine merchant will no longer be appeased by promises.

PIPPA WARE
AUGUST 1993

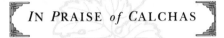

[IN PRAISE of CALCHAS]

Rupert "The Nose" Frobisher, on hearing that I was preparing to compile this little compendium of my wisdom, sent me the following passage, which he claims (if I read his crooked hand aright) was had by him from some brewer of his acquaintance.

Calchas, the Homeric soothsayer, died of laughter. The tale is that a fellow in rags told him he would never drink of the grapes growing in his vineyard, and added, if his words did not come true he would be the soothsayer's slave. When the wine was made, Calchas, at a great feast, sent for the fellow, and laughed so incessantly at the non-fulfilment of the prophecy that, before he had raised a cup to his lips, he died.

Hardly a thigh-slapper of a yarn, of course, but nevertheless – as the sacred Aunt might have it – jolly apostate, what?

FREDDIE DUFF-WARE
AUGUST 1928

PART ONE

FUN *at* the TABLE

EMPTY EGGS

Start with the simple ones, as the prophet said. My second cousin on my mother's side, now the staid Mrs Priscilla Banks-Gore but in those days generally known as that-blasted-Pris-what's-she-done-now, used to perform this prank every single morning as the guests wallowed in the kidneys and kedgeree at Reekington Towers. I blame her father and his Progressive Views for not having the sense to banish her to the nursery for the duration. However, since the only other thing which the blasted child gave me was an embarrassing dose of the mumps, I feel no guilt in reproducing her *culinary jape* here.

If like a curate you have a boiled egg with your matutinal repast, retain the scooped-out shell and substitute it deftly, inverted, in place of an untrammelled egg resting in the cup of one of your elders and betters while he or she is otherwise distracted. Naturally the victim, on returning whey of face to the groaning board, will assume the object to be a Real Egg, and plunge his or her spoon in with as much will as can be mustered at that hour of the day.

Even the Dreaded Aunts took to breakfasting in their beds when staying at Reekington Towers.

CONDIMENTAL BREAKFAST

*M*ost of the prandial jollifications outlined in this monograph associate themselves with the Breakfast Table: up with the lark is the best time for larks, as I think it was Socrates had it. It's at brekkers time that our victims' awarenesses are for obvious reasons at their dullest, so that they're least likely to notice that Mischief is Afoot.

Exchanging condiments is one of the basic capers, but nonetheless mirth-provoking for that. Filling the sugar-caster with salt and the salt-cellar with sugar is de rigueur to the extent that you can often fool your guests by not doing so. It can be hard to button the old lip as they confidently sprinkle their sausages from the salt-cellar. Baking soda in place of

salt is good, especially if your guests must soon be journeying. Curry powder in place of the pepper leads certitudinously to howls of merriment, but my own favourite is to replace the mustard with a dollop of thick CUSTARD.

The morning after a particularly zestful night, I once saw the Duke of Bradborough eat an entire plateful of thus-smeared kidneys and not even notice!

HOT MARMALADE

urveyors of *exotic spices* and condiments are certainly worth investigation for items that look like one thing but are wittily another. If a member of the fouler sex, don't be put off by the fact that you're likely to be the only gentleman in an establishment otherwise patronized exclusively by matrons. Pass the whole thing off with a breezy air by saying that you are shopping on behalf of your Aunt, currently bedridden with cholera, or something, and you'll soon have the place to yourself.

Cayenne pepper and *chilli powder* are a young blade's friends. Either of them can be stirred dextrously into the thinner forms of marmalade until their presence is absolutely undetectable or at least to the eye. To the old taste-buds it's something else ENTIRELY, of course.

Last St Swithin's Day the face of my apoplectic Godfather, the Sabre-Toothed Brigadier, became immediately what was by general consensus an even deeper shade of the imperial colour on sinking half a slice of hot-marmaladed toast into his bear-trap maw. We needed three buckets of water to restore him to his customary puce and a fourth to stop the steam coming out of his ears.

STICKY MOMENTS

*G*lue, as the bard once remarked, is the prankster's pal, and nowhere is this more true than in the devising of racy wheezes for the morning collation.

The fundamental necessity, without which no breakfast can be considered complete, is the fixation of Saucers to Cups. Indeed, after a time, your guests, as they prod the various articles on the table in front of them nervously before settling down to tuck into whatever viands may have been left unadulterated, may become quite upset if you haven't performed this basic function for them. Much the same goes for

spoons and saucers, salt-cellars and tablecloths, ladles and sideboards, and whatnot – even chair-seats.

My own cardinal rule is this: STRIKE FIRST, before they even get to the breakfast table! It is gruelling to rise as the cock croweth, but the dedicated spreader of joy is made of stern stuff, and not averse to the occasional grue. Creep the dawn corridors with all the furtive stealth of a Bolshevik spy, *pot* of *glue* in hand, and attend to the freshly polished shoes outside each door.

I need hardly add that you should be circumspect in your choice of glue. **Flour paste** is ideal, being removable in the course of time. Avoid wood glues and so on like the plague. Some fatheads may be humourless enough to present you with bills for laundry and the like, or stick you with the replacement of shoes and socks.

HOBBLING

s has already been adverted, breakfast is not the meal at which one's average hom sap is at his most percipient, as anyone with a vested interest in stirring up the old mirth glands will know. None of your fellow kidney-stuffers is liable to notice should you drop your napkin ring to the floor and spend an *infernally* long time picking the dashed thing up again. Of course, you're doing more than fetching the offending object; rather, you're scuttling around unseen under Cover of

the Cloth, like the proverbial cat on the h.t.r. Averting your gaze from any nether limbs of a feminine persuasion, you're pouncing on the shoes of the male scoffers, *knotting* the opposing Laces together with all the zeal and dexterity of a card-sharp on the rampage.

Better still is the use of the

Duff-Ware Extrapolation, whereby you link the laces of neighbouring diners to each other. Should one then attempt to effect his escape from the Trough in advance of the other – having, perhaps, just encountered a faceful of Hot Marmalade (see page 14) – DELICIOUS CALAMITY is almost certain to ensue.

RUBBER GOODS

The better class of emporia today has special departments geared to the wiles of the jazz age where any smartly dressed young fellow can lay hands on all sorts of accoutrements for the outlay of at most a few shekels. Foremost of all has to be the rubber sausage, which determinedly resists even the most forthright stab of the hungry fork, instead zipping from the breakfast platter with the speed of a squeezed grape-pip.

Other rubber foods worthy of your attention are: bananas (unpeel-

able), cheese (unsliceable), chickens (uncarvable), gravy (unspoonable) and toast (unchompable). Also efficacious when breakfast threatens to be too tranquil are rubber implements – spoons, forks and the like – as well as those available with discreetly positioned hinges and holes.

For dinners at the club, however, pride of place must go to the rubber bread roll. This dazzles your fellows in the fray, who, confident that your throw has wildly missed them, sit up straight again, smiling smugly until caught on the back of the head by the ricochet.

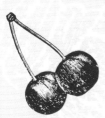

Editors Note: This jape, though amusing at adult weekend parties, is considered quite unsuitable for CHILDREN or in the company of TEETOTALLERS and should not in such circumstances be attempted.

TREACHEROUS COFFEE

*N*ever let it be said that a Duff-Ware overindulges in the headier liquids, or takes pleasure in inebriation for its own sake. At the same time, it cannot be said that a Duff-Ware will be remiss in his duty on those occasions where the bubbly stuff or other ambrosias must be quaffed with a will; I refer of course to celebrations of Birth, Marriage, Death and other Constitutional Landmarks, such as the fact that there's a vowel in the month. Which leads me – indirectly – to the subject of **VODKA**.

As the more adventurous soul will have discovered, this sturdy East European spirit has no flavour, colour or odour: the first you know of its potency is normally when the back of your skull hits the ceiling at the same moment as your body hits the carpet. This is *précisément*, as the French would have it, the property that endears the stuff so to the merry-maker. As the coffee pot steams tantalizingly on the straining breakfast sideboard, it's the work of but a moment to decant into it half a bottle of the fiery liquor. The breakfasters may notice that their copious drafts of the beverage are a little odd, if you know what I mean, but they'll blame the kitchen until they try to rise from their seats, at which they'll discover themselves incapacitated.

Timing's the thing. I once caught the Vicar on a Sunday morning. Later on, in place of a sermon, he gave us a rendition of the juicier passages of the Song of Solomon to the tune of Colonel Bogey…

THE CANDLELIT SWAREE, OR BLUE MURDER!

There comes a time in every chap's life when his gentleman's gentleman must perforce be granted a temporary absence from his duties. For those dire periods the provision of victuals can become something of a problem. Either one can dine at the club, or, if of a bolder disposition, one can essay to master the mysteries of the kitchen oneself. You will be surprised how easy it is to make a sandwich, or what have you, once you've laid hands on the bread and the scissors. Better still is to have your man prepare various dishes for you before he goes, so that all you have to do is remember to light the gas.

You can make a jolly time of it by inviting your friends along to a *Special Candlelit Swaree*, to be laid on by you. The more of the old firewater you lay on, too, the less likely there is to be complaints about your culinary endeavours, and the better the final effect of the prank you've got up your sleeve. Follow my drift, kind reader?

The other thing you must require your man to do before his departure for the exotic luxuries of his holiday domain is to purchase for you some vials of Food Colouring – bilious greens, shrieking yellows, gore reds and, most particular to our requirements, **Royal Blue**. Sling the stuff into the boiling cauldrons before you serve up. In the gloom of the candles' somnolent glow your perfidy will be undetectable, but then, as the assembled stalwarts near the end of the dish, you flick on the lights and – *Blue* soup, *Blue* bubbly, *Blue* fish – you can take your pick, but I've always found that blue macaroni is the best to ensure that it's call-for-the-paper-bags time.

Nuggets

☞ Don't just press someone's door bell and run away. Use a strip of sticking plaster to fasten it down.

☞ Pop a pair of well-aged kippers into a big brown envelope and post 'em to the victim of your choice. Think of how in-demand he'll be when the neighbours smell their letters that day!

☞ A nice big dollop of raspberry jam in a hat should make its presence known to the wearer about a minute and a half after he (or she) donned the doctored tile.

☞ A small quantity of bouquets garnis in the tea-caddy will go a long way.

☞ Put some cold tea in a whisky decanter and serve your pals accordingly: see who's the first to pluck up the courage to say: "Look here, dash it, old boy!"

USEFUL FOODSTUFFS

*Here are some items that should
be on the shelf of
every practical joker*

Powdered Ginger
Hotter than you think it is!
Stirs easily into soup.

Mustard
Ideal for doctoring chocolates, especially those elaborate truffle-style things that tend to get handed around when the Yuletide log's a-blazing, etcetera. Just open up the base of each item, scoop out the filling, replace it with mustard, replace the base, and, if need be, use a heated knife-blade to smooth over the rough edges. Do a whole boxful and give it to a pair of honeymooners!

Raisins and Currants

Mock up a sheet of fly-paper (on no account use the real stuff – it's poisonous) by lightly sticking a scattering of the dried ones to it using flour paste. Wait until everyone's eating and then leap to your feet with a cry of "By Jove! I'm ravenous today!" Haul down the jolly old "fly-paper", brush the "dead flies" off onto a plate, and pop a handful of them down the hatch before anyone can stop you!

Pepper

Ground white pepper is almost as versatile an ally as glue, although in a different way. Every drawer in the guest bedroom should receive a light dusting as a matter of course, as should the geraniums and other pot plants – anything, in short, that the inquisitive nose might sniff. Your own handkerchief should have some within its folds, so that you may whip it out and shake it as if preparatory to blowing your own nose, thereby showering all the goofs around you with such a sufficiency of the stuff that they set to sneezing.

A Cake of Soap

Either white or yellow will do, as long as it doesn't have the maker's mark on it. Just pop it on the cheese-board when no one's looking, and let matters take their obvious course.

Ice Cream, Ice Cubes

Well, I ask you, what else are necklines made for?

PART TWO

HOME AND HEARTH

*(jolly preferably
someone else's)*

APPLE-PIE BEDS

*V*isitors to the various Ware and Duff-Ware establishments around the country have been known to retire for the night grim of visage and with circular saw in hand. Such are the antics of the younger sprogs of my perhaps over-extended family. For myself, I gave up the art of the Apple-pie Bed years ago in search of more ambitious stunts. However, I include this brief discussion of the topic for the sake of comprehensiveness.

The basic technique is as *simple* as Charlie Stross-Puffworthy's brain, which means that it is simplicity itself. Starting with a made bed, strip off the bedspread, quilt, blankets and top sheet, leaving the bottom sheet and mattress in place. Fold the top sheet in half across the middle and tuck one of its two short edges under the mattress, as if it were the upper edge of the bottom sheet. Lay the blankets back on the bed, turn back the free short edge of the top sheet over the blankets in the normal way, and then tuck in the whole assemblage all round as usual. The bed now looks as if it's been made up in the *CUSTOMARY FASHION*. Throw on the pillows and quilt and bedspread, and the trap is set.

For a more durable result, sew up one of the folded sides of the top sheet, and also sew the lower edges of the top sheet to the bottom.

FOAMING AT THE MOUTH

Atoothbrush left on its own is a toothbrush desirous of tampering: rendered into Latin, this would make a *FINE FAMILY MOTTO* – and certainly a better

one than the Duff-Wares' Labor Omnia Vincit, which has remained for generations un-translated. Some day one of us will get round to it, I have no doubt.

In the moments before dinner is served, while the gathering are knocking back their snorts like there's no tomorrow, you are to sneak away on some excuse or other, and dash round the guest bedrooms with a brick of plain white kitchen soap in your hand. But this is no ordinary soap! You should have left it for some hours in advance sitting in a shallow pool of water, so that one side of it has become *sludgy*. It is through this side that you wish to run the bristles of your pals' gnasher-scratchers, washing off any visible excess under the tap. Only a very LITTLE SOAP need be left on the stubbles of the brush, remember: the taste of carbolic goes a long way, especially when mixed in with the less subtle flavours of peppermint and late-night Cognac.

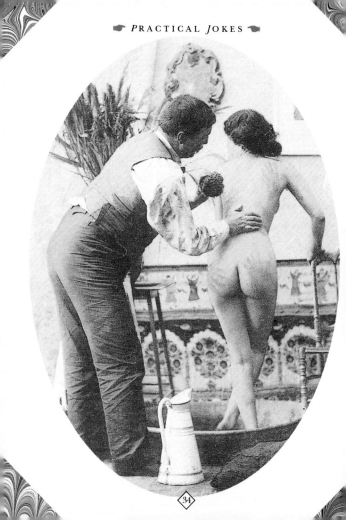

DIRTY HANDS

oap's wonderful stuff, y'know. Didn't use to think so at school, but we're all young at least once. The most *absolutely fascinating* thing about it is that it can be split up and then moulded back together again. Get hold of a thin, part-used Cake of Soap and, using the sharpest knife you can lay hands on without doing yourself an injury, cut it into two even thinner halves. Now NICK OUT a little cavity or two in one of the inner surfaces, and fill it up with soot, or black ink, or dark-brown food colouring. Then use plenty of pressure to make the two halves adhere to each other again, and leave the doctored cake in the downstairs water closet.

It may take some days before the soap is worn down enough through use for your preparations to attain their glorious consequence, but attain it in due course they will.

DIRTY EVERYTHING

*I*n books, especially books of schoolboy stories, you often find pictures of water-filled buckets precariously perched on the tops of doors, so that the next person to come in through the affected portal will, it is hoped, be *drenched* from head to foot, and everyone will have a jolly good thigh-slap. But years of research have taught this investigator that there are two main flaws with such a wheeze: item 1, that it's (regrettably) too dangerous – since the descending bucket might break a chap's neck; and item 2, that it is almost impossible to rig the whole thing up. I do not believe that anyone has ever managed it outside the pages of a book.

But the principle is a jolly good one. Rather than a bucket of water, use instead an open paper bag containing as much *SOOT* as you can stuff into it. If the bag is deep and the paper of which it is made reasonably stiff, you can prop the bag at an angle between the top of the *slightly ajar* door and the wall, so making sure that the load doesn't fall off in the wrong direction (as it otherwise has a habit of doing) when the door is opened.

Experiment with paper bags. Those made of shiny paper are sometimes glued together strongly enough that they can be made to hold water for longish spells: once you find the right marque, you can use water in place of soot.

These are, for obvious reasons, larks to be performed in other people's establishments, rather than your own.

UNEXPECTED SHOWERS

till on the topic of soot, I'm reminded of another simple prank. Whenever the joint is jumping with people there's sure to be a collection of brollies in the stand. Now, the point about an umbrella is that it is only ever opened when it is just about to be used: otherwise it is kept tightly furled. Well, not quite always, because you will need to unfurl

your guests' assortment in order to load each of them with a handful of soot, so that next time they (the chumps) are out and Zeus cuts up rough, it's up with the umbrella... and down with the soot!

Oddly, confetti makes an even better substitute. When wet, it's absolute murder to get the stuff off the old togs, and of course its presence means that until you can get rid of it you're likely to be followed along the street by platoons of raucous small boys...

Nuggets

☞ *Cigars were made to be tampered with. In preparation break off the end of a few match heads, then empty some tobacco out of the end of a cigar. Replace the tobacco with the match heads and cover the end over so that they are completely out of sight. Replace the cigar in its box, then all you have to do is wait for one of those old buffers to light it up...*

☞ *Never let the eye-pieces of telescopes or binoculars go unblacked. The easiest gubbins to use is a sheet of carbon paper, purloined from a stenographer's desk. Simply rub the black round the mounting of the eye-piece, and the next codger to look through it will walk away with a black-ringed eye. An ideal prank for smart race meetings!*

BATH TIME *with a* BANG

*G*etting back to soap – there are other convenient uses for its malleability. Most notably, it can be used to plug things up, most especially *BATH-TAPS*.

You see, the first reaction anyone has on discovering that the tap won't do its stuff is to turn it on even more; then, when nothing happens, to give it a wallop with their fist. At that point the soap usually gives up, and shoots out like the cork out of my nephew Horace's popgun before I finally got my talons on it.

Wise old owls like me bung up only one tap. By the time the bung comes *rocketing* out, there should be enough water in the bath from the other tap for the sap to be at least gently sploshed as the soap impacts.

ITCH! SCRATCH!

Itching powder is stuff of many uses around the house and at the club, in the streets, in emporia, in the halls, at the opera house, on public transport (where there is, as the sainted Aunt knows, little enough else of amusement), in parks, in the dental surgery, at pals' establishments, on cruises – well, just about bally everywhere, in fact. I have scarcely a doubt that, somewhere up in the clouds, after checking people's admission tickets St Peter offers to sell 'em a carton of the stuff under the counter at wholesale prices.

In the sort of quantities the full-time jollifier is liable to require, the commercial stuff can become BLISTERINGLY expensive – especially when it's easy enough to obtain your own for not so much as a bean. The shop powder is in fact nothing more than very finely trimmed BRISTLES shaven from the jowls of fellows.

The Duff-Ware jowls, indeed, offer rather better vegetative produce than any I have found elsewhere. All you need to do is save it carefully after each go with the cut-throat, wash it, and then leave it to dry out thoroughly in the airing cupboard. Friends can often be induced to add their own offerings, and if your requirements are truly gargantuan you can certainly, as has yrs truly, come to some sort of an arrangement with a barber – indeed, the clipping that come from his gadget are possibly even better than the products of your razor.

CREEPY TREATS

Imagine the scene I place before you. Perfectly ordinary sideboard, or so it seems, burdened down with the provender about to be bolted by the assembly. But what is this? A young guest, fingers in her mouth beyond the second knuckle, steam coming out of her ears like geysers, eyes somewhere about a foot in front of her forehead. What has she seen? And why does she swoon, like girls do, when you appear at her side, pick up something from the sideboard, and neck it back with every seeming sign of enjoyment?

The answer to these – and, for all I know, many other – questions is: *MARZIPAN.*
Carving a block of the stuff into a gigantic COCKROACH or TARANTULA is easier than you might think, given a keenish pen-knife and a sharp needle for

the details. Though it might not seem so at first, great big sweaty SPIDERS are easier than beetle-type bugs because no one chooses to look too closely at a *spider*, if you know what I mean. Colouring can be effected with our old friend food colouring, painted on, or even chocolate icing while it's still liquid. Use your imagination, your ingenuity, your creative flair! (Or do as I do, which is to buy the things ready-made.)

THE HEIRLOOM

*M*ost writers of monographs might have been in two minds as to whether to allocate this joke to Part Five: Absolutely Elaborama but we of the Duff-Ware ilk have been granted only the single mind (mine), and so the prank is listed here instead.

Find in one of those frightful *False Antique Shops* some worthless brummagem of an old vase, unchipped, and bring it home with you. Using a hammer, smash it rather carefully, so that it doesn't fly into too many sharp thingies. Then, using paper glue, stick it back carefully together, but not very well: your aim is that it should look whole but in fact be held together by little more than a wing and a prayer.

Next you require a **collapsing** card-table and possibly a piece of

black thread. Most collapsing card-tables collapse all too readily and certainly they can almost always be rigged so that the slightest waft of Boreas's breath will bring them tumbling to the ground ... which in this instance is what you want them to do. Experiment! For the execution of the stunt you're going to have the table by the drawing-room door, the slamming of which should be enough to make it fold up; you may find you have to encourage the collapse by affixing the thread unobtrusively between the door and one of the table-legs.

And who should arrive at your doorstep but Mr. G.Oof, the least favourite of your circle. However, today you are actually pleased to see his doleful mug. As he stands in your drawing-room sucking his boater like a namby, talk about this and that, including the fantastically valuable piece of MING that you have just inherited – been in the family for a zillion years. You end by telling Mr. G. Oof that on no account must he touch the revered artefact, and then on some pretext or other leave him alone in the room, slamming the door behind you as you leave …

PART THREE

OUT
AND
ABOUT

SIGNS TO THE AFT

*T*he classic alfresco prank is of course the affixing to a fellow's back of an instructional notice. When I was at the old establishment the practice was always to letter the notice with the simple message as follows: KICK ME. Later on, when civilization had put a veneer of courtesy and sophistication over our youthful hearts, we expanded this rather to read:

> I SAY, WOULD YOU MIND AWFULLY IF I ASKED
> YOU TO EXERT YOURSELF SUFFICIENTLY TO
> RAISE THE OLD NETHER LIMB AND PLANT YOUR
> BOOT IN MY FUNDAMENT?

Not so pithy, as you'll understand, but showing the merits of a Classical education.

Now that I move in somewhat ritzier society, I realize that such exhortations are passé, that they lack a certain je ne comprends pas, *if you like. Much more effective and* nouveau, *I've found, is:*

KISS ME

❤ ❤ ❤ ❤ ❤ ❤ ❤ ❤

SHAKING HANDS

By the above I do not mean the natural symptoms exhibited by those who cannot recall how they got home the night before. Instead my allusion is to the repulsive common practice, on greeting or leaving one's fellow mortal, of grasping the appropriate appendage hotly and waving it about frenetically as if trying to get it dry.

I understand that some make great play out of buying little electronic gadgets that can be concealed in the palm, so that the victim is given an unexpected *buzzing jolt*. Well, all I can say is that you would have thought that their Master Edison might have found something better to occupy his brain-cells.

My own preference as a reward for those who insist on pawing me is, beforehand, to seek in the garden an example of our old friend *Limax commonalis*, the Garden Slug, or more simply, but less effectively, a peeled grape. Handling the fellow gently, roll him about in your hands until your palm is coated with a goodly measure of the **mucus** these beasts exude, and then, jauntily brollied and monocled as the occasion demands, set off for the street. If someone insists on being shaken by the hand, that's their fate sealed. (The same goes for any of those ghastly flappers or maiden Aunts that refuse to let you go without a suffocating embrace.)

As the Victim Cringes with revulsion from the residue you've left on them, don't forget to remark cheerfully that you've got a too too *frightful* cold at the present.

RAINING BOUQUETS

Young nephews are useful for very few things. In fact, their sole perceptible advantage is that they tend to carry about with them the sort of valuable accoutrements that those of more sober years can obtain with only very considerable difficulty and embarrassment. I refer, of course, to such items as fake inkblots, plastic spiders, pea-shooters and – de rigueur – naturally-grown disreputable handkerchiefs. For the purposes of our current endeavour, however, what you must purloin the next time you see one of the little blighters is his water pistol – the more powerful and capacious the better, for you want to be able to deliver a positively diluvial blast.

As you'll have noticed, a chap can't walk down the street with a bunch of flowers in his grapple, without all and sundry assuming that it's destined for some loved one rather than – as is inevitably the truth

– his mother. Or even an Aunt, such are the exigencies of needful flattery. I digress. As I say, whenever you're perambulating flower-laden, heading about your own private business, people seem to think that the very presence of the aforementioned blossoms permits them a much more intimate intercourse with than they would otherwise dare. In particular, one and all, they will insist on sticking their noses

into the top of the foliage and inhaling as if their very lives depended on it.

It is at that moment, Fellow Spirit, that your finger tightens on the trigger of the water pistol that you have concealed at the base of the stems …

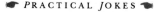
A FATE *A* JOLLY SIGHT WORSE THAN DEATH
I can assure you

ere's a gag that demands
Complete and Total
Anonymity on your
part – not a whiff
of your in-
volvement must reach the
outside world, or you'll
jolly well find yourself
with gaping gaps in your
circle of friends in no
long order.

Paying by **cash**, book
a classified advertisement
in the "Engagements"
column on the front of
the newspaper, and
express joy that, say, Miss
Rosemary "Binksie"
Grapple-Kaveney, dearly
beloved daughter of,
etcetera, etcetera, is due to
be hitched to the Rt. Hon.

Malcolm Fitter-Couch, Esq. & Bar, upstanding younger son of the Late Brigadier, etcetera, etcetera – or any other equally inappropriate coupling of your acquaintance – and simply sit back and wait for public gossip to do the rest!

WITH ALL DUE THANKS
TO MR. BELL

*B*efore the hour of noon, there are few more despicable inventions that of Mr. Alexander Graham Bell. After the Sun has hoisted itself over the yardarm is, of course, another matter entirely – how else would one hear of impromptu bashes? Even then, the telephone can be a confoundedly disconcerting item, because of the habit one's associates have of leaving incomprehensible messages for one when one is not actually in situ, as it were.

But every clod has a sillier lining, as my Classics Tutor was fond of observing, and the said remark can (albeit with some considerable difficulty) be applied to the gas-engine. For you can be the one to leave confusing messages for someone else, for a change. Assure yourself that Nostrils Gee (or whoever else you plan to victimize) is safely out of his cage, and then, adopting vocal contortions appropriate to the moment, ring his ménage in various guises, express dismay at his absence, and leave a message desiring that he telephone you on his return. Give your name and number, of course ... or, rather, a name and a number. When he obeys instructions he will find some nasty surprises, as the number you have left is in fact that of a famous establishment, and the name unduly fitting, so that he finds himself asking for: **Mr. Lyons** at the Park Zoo or **Mr. Flushing** at the Sewage Works.

Use your imagination to invent more and more of these!

Mr Stark or Mr. Raven, please? *Kennington Home for the Mentally Infirm*

Could I speak to Mr. Ashe? *Golders Green Crematorium*

Is Mr. D. Rip there, please? *Acme Plumbing Services*

Mr Wheel, please? *Smithsonian Institute*

I'd like to speak to Mr. Lions *The Park Zoo*

SURVEYING

All you need for this business is a measuring-tape. Accost some unfortunate type in the street and ask him if he'd mind awfully doing you a bit of a favour. Explain that you're a gentleman surveyor, and that you've been asked to measure the adjacent building; however, your employee has failed to appear for work – the malingerer will be getting his cards in the morning, you can asseverate – but in the meantime you'd be eternally grateful if the flat-headed *bozo* could take one end of your measuring-tape, just for a minute or so.

You may even offer him some sort of pecuniary reward once the task is done, if that is the cast of his Piggish Little Eye.

Exhorting him to keep the tape taut at all times, retreat around the nearest corner, paying the tape out as you go. Once there, waylay some equally **antediluvian**-looking specimen and impart to his sluggardly grey matter a message of almost identical import. If he could just hold this *tape taut* for a moment while you attend to something?

Then, of course, you simply hoof it to some suitable observation post.

BLOOMF!

A harmless and handy tool for any joker is that of the flour bomb. For this you require a paper bag – the thinner the better – and surprisingly small quantities of sieved flour: anything more than a couple of spoonfuls and your bomb is likely to be a wet squib. Pop a handful in the bag, and twist the loose corners of the bag *very loosely indeed* – just enough so that the flour will be retained when the bag is inverted.

Then it's up to your high window, and the mayhem begins! Hold the bag inverted for dropping, and this time aim directly at the passers-by beneath you.

Nuggets

Get hold of a few bottles of concentrated (edible) food colouring – I prefer blue, but red and green are other efficacious hues – and decant them into the cold-water tank at a pal's establishment. Or you could pop the stuff into the cistern in the Smallest Room, so that soon the company start urgently enquiring after each other's health.

Saw down a pea-shooter to half or less of its length, so that it can be hidden easily in your hand. Take it with you everywhere you go – but most especially to dull operas sung in silly languages. Use grains of rice or barley rather than the customary split peas or lentils: being smaller and pale they're a lot harder for the victim to find about his person, and so identify what struck him.

PART FOUR

NOT
for the
GENTLER SEX

UNFLUSHED WITH
SUCCESS

I have heard it said more than once: "Duff-Ware flincheth not from the difficult bits." In this section of what I am pleased to call my monograph I propose, therefore, to include some of the less seemly antics and capers. In short, this section is **Hot Stuff**.

While I myself am not prudish – within reason, of course – and I assume that you yourself are not averse to facing the more brutal of bodily functions, the truth is that virtually everybody else in the world is. *Squeamish* about such things, I mean. That's the Chink in their Armour.

Here's an old but much loved favourite, not only useful for getting rid of unwanted house-guests. If you examine the cistern in the Smallest Room you'll find that an integral part of its workings is a connecting-whatjamacallit between the lever arm from which the chain hangs and the mechanism proper. It's the work of but a moment and a pair of pliers to disconnect this rod. Make sure that the invader of your hospitality is plied with plenty of tea.

Fishface Crawthorne says it's cruel to leave 'em locked away struggling for more than half an hour. Myself, I always give 'em forty-five minutes, at the end of which they normally find they're urgently needed elsewhere, and make a swift getaway before you Discover Their Shame.

THE WHOOPEE BALLOON

𝒲ho would have guessed how many hours of merry mayhem could be caused by nothing more elaborate than a child's balloon and a button? Puff up the balloon in the customary fashion and then, with your fingers holding the neck so that the air can't come rushing out, insert a largish flattish button into the opening, so that the rubber is stretched nice and tight around it. If you now relax the pressure of your fingers a little, the balloon should produce a satisfactorily coarse noise as the air struggles to escape past the button. (In fact, if you let go of the balloon altogether, it should drift away, whining vulgarly, and dash around like something demented.)

Small balloons are the best for use, because they can the more easily be secreted in coat pockets and the like, and brought out discreetly at the necessary moment. The technique of use is to carry one on your person when going to attend some suitably long-faced gathering, sneak off into a quiet corner and inflate the article. Stand near to the person of greatest pomposity – a Bishop for preference – with the balloon behind out of sight, and, at a suitable point in the Great Man's discourse, allow your balloon to let rip. Shoot a daggered, disdainful glance at the pontificator, and stalk away with a look of disgust on the old physog.

TOOTHSOME

*H*ere's a tasteless joke – too strong for the stomach of the average gel. Purchase from the confectioner of your choice a bagful of those little white peppermint drops, Just before coming to the dinner table, pop about half a dozen of the mints into your cheek. Then, rather than throw your bread roll, pretend to take a bite from it and give an agonized cry of: "By G–, but this bread's stale!" So saying, give a sort of piteous cough, and spit out the mints like bullets into the empty plate in front of you.

With practice, you may find you can manage to keep some tomato sauce in your cheek as well as the sweets.

68

Nuggets

Another simple, but nonetheless effective joke, is to sew up the ends of the sleeves and trouser legs of some old duffer's pyjamas.

Worse than any stinkbomb is the elaborate act of sewing some fresh prawns into the curtain linings of your worst enemy. The purloining of the prawns may seem an expensive act at the time, but the whiff they provide after a few days is hard to match. Old Duff-Ware always advised that this joke should carry a warning, due to its longlasting effect and the fact that the curtains definitely won't recover.

The age-old trick of a hairbrush hidden down the bottom of a bed is one of the simplest and easiest tricks to execute. A cold hot-water bottle has an equally unpleasant feel to it.

"AFORE YE GO"

Another item obtainable from the chemist's shop is stuff called laxative chocolate – produced, no doubt, for grim old *battleaxes* who don't draw the line at chewing broken bottles but do draw it (the line) at being seen to require Epsom salts in order to shift the evidence. All you have to do is buy a few bars, break them up into their constituent lumps, put them in a bowl, and leave them lying around somewhere not too obtrusive at a party. Human greed will do the rest, eh?

A MATTER OF CONVENIENCE

$\mathscr{M}$uch mirth can be derived from the judicious preparation and positioning of information signs that are in fact as fake as many a modern actress's vital statistics. If, therefore, you put a neatly lettered plate saying **MUSEUM:** Admission 9.00–5.00 on a pal's front door, you can be sure that only moments will pass before

a deluge of rubbernecks will be pounding the panels demanding entrance. Alternatives include the one the eagle-eyed reader will have guessed from the heading of this page, **MADAME GIOVANNA:** Romany Fortune-Teller and, of course, **HOUSE OF ILL REPUTE:** This Week Only – Free Samples.

A *B* IN THE *O*

*O*ne of the iffiest pranks to reach my ears in recent years has been, despite its questionable taste, one actually perpetuated by a gel – Bogbrush Bell's dippy sister Christine, none other. Seems she was getting fed up to the rearmost fangs with the way that Chuffy Stewart was boasting all over town about the way she dewed in the old orbs every time his name was mentioned, acted winsome in his presence, and spoke of going into a nunnery if she could not have his heart. All balderdash, of course. So one day the gel turns up on his doorstep while he's entertaining his f. and m. and various other relatives to drinks, a balloon stuffed up the front of her ensemble, wringing her hands and with tears running down her dimples, to announce to all and sundry that "she was only a poor gel and he done her wrong". Loud aghastment in all directions, pince-nezes dropping into the fizz like flies into jampots, etcetera, Chuffy doing his best to explain that digits had been left unlaid, and so forth. Just as the shotguns are being produced the doughty lass pulls out a hairpin from her scalp and leaves the gathering with a farewell Bang.

PART FIVE

ABSOLUTELY ELABORAMA

"BUT *I* THOUGHT IT WAS *THURSDAY*!"

Again this is a joke requiring a group of Like Spirits and a single victim. Before the bozo arrives on the scene you must decide what day of the week it is – any day you wish, except the day it actually is, of course. If it happens to be a Sunday, and you know that the goof is of that unfortunate class which needs to work in an office or something frightful during the week, then decide among yourselves that it is "really" a Monday.

Then, when the fellow shows up, behave to all intents and purps as you would were it to be a **Monday.** For example, you could remark upon the excellence of the sermon that the Bishop delivered the day before.

This ploy can be especially effective with house-guests if you carry it out over the breakfast table, when one's wits are anyway still a bit on the disorientated side.

GHOST: *I*

*O*nce again, as before it doesn't take an Einstein to guess the setup: bunch of blades and flappers, odd geezer out, decide the stratagem beforehand, etcetera. This time, though, you will need to do some preparation in advance.

"The truth is", you will say earnestly (I find that the simple act of polishing the old monocle as I talk always adds a certain touch of seeming earnestness to my discourse, but you may have your own modi operandii), that the room in which you have all gathered is reputed to be haunted — not that you yourself believe a word of such tosh, you assure the company, but you thought they'd be amused by the tale. Apparently (you're still boshing on) the ghost of Hector the Dead Rector stalks the pile every 28th of February (or whatever the date perchances) and reveals its presence only to those who are about to die or, worse, marry.

Just at that point, the lights go off and on (this is where your colleague is starting to do his stuff). The goof naturally says something like: "I say, you fellows. I could have sworn that there was a brief illuminatory lapse." All of you look blank, however: you've noticed nothing. There's a colossal bang-crash from behind the sofa (a pin and a balloon will do the trick); but, once again, no one except the by now sweating ape notices anything. Bugle-calls, rattlings from the walls, steam pouring in through the keyhole – all can be arranged using a little of your ingenuity, yet you and the rest of the party are Utterly Oblivious to all, carrying on as if nothing were amiss.

If you wish, you can mention *apropos* of nothing that your least presentable Aunt has recently taken to looking broody every time the goof's name is mentioned.

GHOST: *II*

*H*ere you need to have briefed a good-size circle of jollifiers in advance. One day the selected turkey will inevitably call upon one of your number – for the sake of argument, let us assume that the host in question is yourself. When Mr. G. Oof appears at the portal you must gasp, clutch your heart, stagger to a chair, etcetera, clearly going apoplectic with dread and amaze. When he asks if perhaps last night's oysters are taking their revenge, stutter out convincingly that no, no, it's not that: rather, that you know for absolute f. that he – Mr. G. Oof, no less – is DEAD. It is his spectre to which you must be talking ...

This news is likely to fill the average chap with a degree of surprise. I mean to say, normally you'd expect to notice having popped off. He'll assure you, of course, that reports of his demise are somewhat on the exaggerated side, and ask you where you got the guff from. At which you say that it was Niffy MacPherson who told you, and stagger chokingly to Master Bell's invention. Niffy, of course, will stammer that you must be grievously mistaken, old Oofers certainly gone like a candle in a gale, went to the funeral himself, etcetera. You get the same sort of reply when you telephone Eggflip O'Sullivan, Knickerbockers Barrett and even Whatd'yesay Langford.

At about this time you should start trying to drive off the hapless Mr. G. Oof with a Cross ...

FOR SALE!

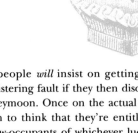

If people *will* insist on getting hitched up, it's their own blistering fault if they then discover that they have to go on honeymoon. Once on the actual honeymoon, of course, they seem to think that they're entitled to blight the lives of the fellow-occupants of whichever luckless hotel they descend on by spending all their waking hours **simpering.** Such loathsome specimens can hardly complain if they return home to one or two nasty surprises, eh? Thought you'd agree.

A suitable welcome for the cooing turtledoves' return is the discovery that their darling little nook has been put on the market. It's the matter of a moment to organize the purloinment and preparation of a suitable "FOR SALE" sign to go in the front garden. Advertisements in the local rags must be placed surreptitiously, of course, and signed with a suitably plausible Estate Agency name:

Rampton & Shackle, for example. The telephone number given in the advertisement must be, of course, your own, newly changed for the purpose; waiting in for the calls from prospective buyers is somewhat of a bind, but colleagues can be instructed to play their part. Obtaining the keys need not be too much of a difficulty – call on the unsuspecting relative to whom the keys have been entrusted, and fool them with some ruse.

By the date of the young flutterwings' return, negotiations for the sale should be well advanced. Don't forget to have your telephone number changed back to its original.

SURPRISE PARTIES: THE DUFF-WARE

For a while it was *plus la rage* to throw surprise parties for returning honeymooners – certainly it was no more than they deserved, to arrive back on the threshold and find half a hundred merry-makers throwing streamers and buns. But such activities have become somewhat *passé;* moreover, the last

thing you want at a decent thrash is the sight of two young moonstruck morons watching the bluebirds flutter out of each other's eyes. It is for both of these superlatively excellent reasons that I propose a much improved Development of the Original Surprise Party. Which is:

Have the party before the ghastly couple get home!

Yes. Throw the biggest and wildest binge that Anyone Can Remember, with raucous music and quarts of the Essential Stuff for every guest; all the better if the neighbours are moved to send letters of complaint. And leave the house as you would wish someone else to find it: bottles and fag-ends everywhere, half-eaten *quiches* stuffed down the backs of the upholstery, commodes irreparably blocked, beds rumpled to the point of destruction and garments of an intimate nature littering every room.

Last but not least, leave a thank-you note for a Truly Spiffing Wizard Bash, and *make sure absolutely everyone signs it.*

'WE'VE COME TO STAY'

There is nothing more chilling even to the soundest constitution than those dreaded words "we've come to stay".

The traditional **Introductory Letter** is the excellent precursor of this unfeeling prank, inflicting the most dubious of short-term acquaintances upon one's chums at a safe distance from any

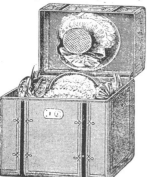

repercussion. Achieve instant far-reaching revenge with the simplest of notes – or, updated to its modern form – the provision of personal telephone numbers to the unsuitable and invariably thick-skinned traveller!

With the aid of a co-operative friend, unknown to the victim, this cruel jest can be put into immediate action, with the benefit of receiving a later hilarious blow-by-blow report of the reaction of your stricken-faced erstwhile chum. An antipodean colleague known worldwide for a propensity to settle for extended spells upon the slightest excuse, as well as for an intimacy with the long-distance telephone, is a perfect choice for imparting maximum terror. Unwashed hair, excessive

baggage and the absence of a ticket home complete the disguise. A friendly message conveying the good wishes of yourself, received warmly by your unsuspecting pal, is followed by a doorstep visit...

Utilized in its simplest form, this prank is sufficient to strike fear and loathing into otherwise staunch friends and the once-chummiest of aquaintances. Increased twisting of the knife can also be achieved with simple disguise – perhaps the donning of the garb of a seemingly respectable elderly lady, visiting a local dignitary on the invitation of his "nephew"; or a grey-suited foreign visitor descending on the home of one Hopeful for Promotion, on the basis of a "letter" from the Company Director...

THE LETTER OF THE LAW

It has been astutely observed by more than one commentator on life in general that (to paraphrase) *"something in writing is a thing of weight and general soundness"*. This so-human susceptibility is easily manipulated and abused with the creation of 'official' notices, and the distribution of serious-looking memorandums and missives to the unsuspecting.

The memorandum is a powerful weapon in the prankster's armoury, and to guarantee the desired result should always be manufactured on the correct materials. The more time spent on authenticity, the better. For extra effectiveness, always add a little detail at the end. In this note, handed out in the corridors and classrooms of one of our finer schools (by my nephew, actually) at the end of the morning lessons, it was the final sentence which did the trick:

"To celebrate the engagement of Mr Winkle [the headmaster] to Miss Fitzjolly [the matron] a half-day holiday is granted to all pupils this afternoon Please note: homework must still be handed in tomorrow morning."

Similarly a colleague of mine in the Colonial Service got away with the same trick on new recruits. A formally bound booklet labelled, *"Rules and Regulations"*, was left on the desk of the **novices** for their first day, and included, amongst dozens of other nuggets, the following:

Item 3. Health regulations require a urine sample from each new staff member. Please leave this on the desk of your Section head by 9.00 a.m. on your second day of employment (do utilize a well-sealed container).

Item 7. Until you have had your full communications training and assessment course (in week two), you are kindly requested not to answer the telephone.

REMEMBER THE 4 As
1. *Authenticity of manner*
2. *Authenticity of materials*
3. *Authenticity of production*
4. *Always add superfluous/officious detail.*

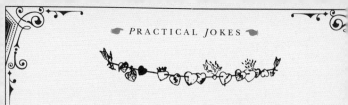
PARADISE LOST

There can be fewer situations more tempting to the serious joker than that of the Intimate Romantic Dinner. For true maliciousness and the callousest of practical jokes, it offers limitless potential.

First, ascertain the full details of the assignation - the venue, the date, the timing. You will need to visit the site ahead for most effective planning. Reserve a special table in the victim's name – then, follow this up with separate bookings for the surrounding tables. It is next a simple

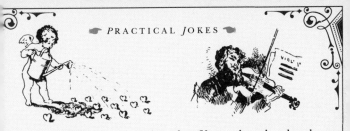

matter of disguise and seating plan. You and a select band of artful colleagues will be arranged at the tables surrounding the unsuspecting couple, who are still innocently gazing into each other's eyes over the flickering candle, etc. etc.

Each party should then proceed to take their turn - a gradually increasing disturbance is generally more effective than an immediate onslaught, allowing a delicious progressive embarrassment of the victims before the hilarious stages of irritation, indignation and fury are achieved ...

One party could be a group of noisy bachelors on a stag night, in a state of advanced inebriation and clumsiness – bread rolls and salt-cellars fly "accidentally" on to the next table, as one member of the party staggers into the lady as she is about to spoon soup into her mouth; open and ribald comments on the couple are indiscreetly aired... The next party could be a married couple in the midst of a loud and outspoken argument... On the adjoining table, over-friendly foreign tourists could interrupt our victims with incessant queries, requesting advice on the menu, the customs to be observed...

The pièce de résistance would be the appearance of a uniformed official, perhaps a "police officer" to issue the gentleman concerned with a warrant for his arrest as the leading suspect of a recent corruption fraud; an obnoxiously pompous "traffic warden" in respect of an illegally parked car; or even a tearful "ex-wife" in a state of advanced pregnancy.

Nuggets

~ In any home that's newly acquired a cat, make up a mixture of lemon juice and vinegar, and dispose puddles of it artistically around the place.

~ In some public, enclosed space – a railway carriage, or the theatre stalls – start scratching yourself furiously and then, apparently, catch a flea. Soon others will be scratching themselves too.

~ A simple trick that always upsets the frosty old aunts and raises a few blushes is to swap over the chaps' nightgowns with those of the old gals.

~ Glue a coin to the road if you want to cause some public humiliation. How the passers-by blush when they realize they have been caught penny-pinching

THE UPSIDE-DOWN ROOM

T his is by far the most elaborate jape I have ever executed. It is both time- and energy-consuming: definitely not for those of faint heart. If you wish to imitate it you will require a deal of money and a number of friends of likewise bubbling spirits. What you and your pals set out to do is to turn an entire room upside-down.

As I muttered, it takes time. Choose a sap who's going to be away on his hols for a while – or perhaps you could save this extra-special little stinker for a brace of honeymooners, for all the good reasons expounded on an earlier page.

First you must select the room that you wish to transform (in the case of the lovebirds, of course, your choice is automatic – assuming the bed isn't too galumphing, for there's a limit to the weight of the furniture you can tackle). You will need oodles of string, screws, screwdrivers,

plaster,
nails, glue,
T- and L-flanges
(bits of metal folded at
angles, with holes punched
through them) and several step-
ladders, plus a few other things I've probably forgotten
about. Plenty of the bubbly to help you on your labours is a good
wheeze, too.

Furniture legs can be affixed to the ceiling by use of the metal flanges
and screws, drilling through carpets and rugs that you have already
nailed into place. Upholstery can be held in place using string, plaster,
needle and thread (knew I'd forgotten something!), etcetera. Glue will
hold items upside-down on to the surfaces of occasional tables and the
like; with a little ingenuity, you can even manage items like magazines
and books left open at the place. Most difficult of all can be arranging
for the ceiling fixtures to stick up from the floor.

When all is done, tidy up very carefully – that's part of the illusion.
Be assured, as you tiptoe away on the final day of your enterprise, that
entering the room will be, for the victim or victims, like entering the
nightmare of the madhouse.

Finis